THE **GARDEN**
BOOK

hamlyn

First published in Great Britain in 1999 by
HAMLYN, a division of
OCTOPUS PUBLISHING GROUP
LIMITED
2-4 Heron Quays, London E14 4JP

This edition published for S.T.I.S. in 1999

ISBN 0 600 59997 3

A CIP catalogue record for this book
is available from the British Library

Produced by Cayfosa
Printed and bound in Spain

CONTENTS

DESIGNING YOUR GARDEN

Quick tips for your ideal garden
4

GARDEN PLANS
Informal rectangular garden 7
Low-maintenance garden 8
Gravel garden 10
Container garden 12

CONSTRUCTION

GARDEN FEATURES
Ponds 14

SURFACES
Decking 17

USING PLANTS

Plant associations 20
Creating a border 30

THEME PLANTS
Ways with roses 36

PLANT SELECTOR
Shrubs for year-round interest
43

Acknowledgements 48

QUICK TIPS
FOR YOUR IDEAL GARDEN

Practicalities

WORK OUT how much you can afford to spend on your new garden.

*   *There is no point thinking up a grand scheme if you can't afford to carry it out.*

Work out how much spare time you have to spend in your garden to maintain it.

*   *If you lead a hectic life, you may well not have a lot of time to garden, in which case, work out a low-maintenance plan for your new garden.*

Ask yourself what you want out of your new garden. Are you a passionate plant collector? Do you have small children? Do you want to grow vegetables as well as flowers? Assess your site and consider what is possible and what is not possible to achieve.

*   *If, for example, you have a shady garden, it's no use having a new design that incorporates large areas of flowerbeds, filled with sun-loving plants. Similarly, if you live in an area of chalky soil, there are certain plants which will not thrive there.*

Ideas

NOW YOU have done all the practical work, start thinking in more detail. Do you want grass or paving? How much border space do you want? More to the point, how much time do you have to keep your borders looking good?

*   *On the whole, paving is easier to maintain than grass, which needs regular mowing. However, borders also need a certain amount of work to look good.*

Once you have roughly divided your garden into areas of paving, grass and borders, or a combination of any two, make a list of features you want.

*   *Go out into your garden and just look around you. Scribble down any ideas that may come to you. Then go inside and imagine what your new garden will look like from both downstairs and upstairs windows.*

If your garden is a difficult shape, such as short and wide or long and thin, try and work out how to disguise this.

*   *Your garden will appear longer than it really is if you have a diagonal layout that leads the eye from a front corner to a back corner. If you want to make your garden seem shorter, divide it into separate 'compartments' linked by a winding path.*

Don't be discouraged by sloping ground; in fact a contoured garden is usually more interesting than a flat one.

*   *Make the most of slopes by having a rockery or waterfall, or even by making a series of terraces and raised beds.*

Putting pen to paper

FIRST MEASURE your garden and transfer your measurements to a sketch.

*   *Measure all the major distances in your garden. It makes it much easier if you take a fixed point, such as the corner of your house, and measure everything you can from there.*

Now make a scale plan so you have a realistic plan of your garden as it is.

*   *The most useful scale to work to is 1 or 2cm to 1m (¼ or ⅛ in to 1ft), depending on how big your garden is and the size of paper. Work on squared or graph paper.*

Once you have a scale plan, you can draw up your ideas.

*   *Mark everything about your new design on your plan so you can carry the scheme out with accuracy and confidence.*

Carrying out your plans

ONCE YOU have decided on your new design and drawn it on your plan, you may need to get professional help with any major soil works or hard landscaping.

*   *Don't try to do everything yourself if you do not have the expertise to do so. In the long run, it is much more time- and cost-effective to get professional help.*

GARDEN PLANS

*Planning your garden is terrific fun.
It's the time to put on your thinking cap
before the hard work begins in earnest.
For some people, this is probably the
most exciting time of all in the process
of creating a new garden.*

This is the time when you can sit
down, pencil in hand, and put your
ideas down on paper. It's the time
to let your imagination run riot.

But careful constructive planning
isn't all about creative instincts. It
also requires a cool head. There are
raw materials to be considered,
lifestyles to be taken into account,
practicalities to be weighed up,
budgets to be calculated. Above all,
there are decisions to be made.

Do you have a small garden or
something rather grander? Do you
want a formal feel to your garden,
or would you prefer something
less geometrical, less orderly? Do
you plan to spend a lot of time
gardening or would you like a
low-maintenance option? Is your
garden square, rectangular or
L-shaped, which gives you maximum
opportunity for springing surprises?
Does your garden take place on just
the one level or are there two, or
more, different levels to be exploited?
Are you content with stone and
concrete, or do you hanker after
something more adventurous?
These are all questions that you
need to ask yourself.

What follows over the next
few pages is a number of different
approaches to drawing up a
garden plan. Take a look at these
and see which of these gardens
approximates most closely to the
raw materials you have to play
with, and which type of garden
comes nearest to your chosen style.

Look upon these plans not as
blueprints to be copied but as
sources of inspiration. See what
takes your fancy and let your
imagination do the rest.

I N F O R M A L
R E C T A N G U L A R
G A R D E N

INFORMAL RECTANGULAR GARDEN

*T*he inclusion of an arresting object within a small garden is an excellent way of detracting the eye from adjacent buildings and into the garden itself. The focal point in this garden is an ornate wrought-iron seat, which leads the eye down the garden. The rather austere rectangular lawn is surrounded by a mass of pretty, shrubby little plants, which together help to soften the overall look of the garden.

❶
FLOWERING SHRUBS

Large shrubs in a small garden must have a long flowering season to justify their space.

❸
STEPS BOUNDED BY RAISED BEDS

The plain, angular line of stone steps can be softened by building raised flower beds on either side.

❷
FOCAL POINT

A pretty, ornate wrought-iron seat, positioned invitingly at the end of a narrow garden, will draw the eye towards it and will beckon visitors to sit on it.

❹
SEMI-CIRCULAR RAISED BED

Siting a semi-circular raised bed under the window links the garden to the house in a curved shape and lifts the flowers nearer to eye-level for people sitting on the terrace.

LOW-MAINTENANCE GARDEN

This garden has a simple, low-maintenance design which is exciting and interesting to look at. The uniform paving is complemented by the curved edge of the pond and raised beds. Different types of stone (bricks and cobbles) have also been used in a stone tapestry-like effect on the ground. There is a tree seat and attractive furniture, both of which add interest.

❸ CENTRAL PAVING PATTERN

The imaginative mix of bricks, cobbles and paving slabs in the central ground area creates a kind of decorative masonry rug.

❶ RAISED POND

A small raised pond may be home to Nymphaea (waterlilies), and it will reflect the surrounding foliage.

❷ SHADY SEAT

The white cast-iron seat around a fast-growing *Ailanthus altissima* tree makes an attractive place to sit in the shade in hot weather.

❹ FLOWERING PLANTS IN POTS

A broad range of plants with different growing requirements can be grown in containers and then positioned in sun or shade.

LOW-
MAINTENANCE
GARDEN

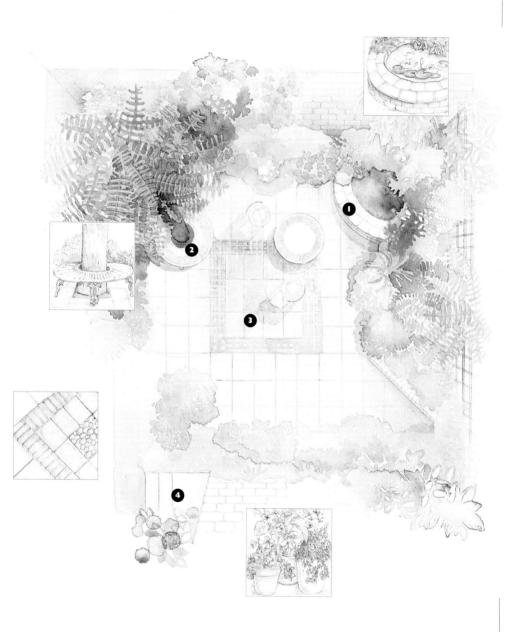

GRAVEL GARDEN

GRAVEL GARDEN

Ιn this design, the hard, clear lines of paving have been softened by an area of light gravel, which also works as an effective foil for the carefully chosen background plants. The colour and texture of the gravel also contrast well with the purple-leaved shrub which dominates the terrace. The height of the plants is accentuated by the smallness of the miniature alpines growing near eye-level in a water butt.

1

LAWN AND GRAVEL

Interesting texture contrasts are provided by a small lawn area surrounded by gravel, the broken surface of the gravel setting off the smooth finish of the lawn. The gravel has to be prevented from straying on to the lawn by a hard edging of stone or timber boards.

3

SUNKEN CONTAINER

A sunken area breaks up a stretch of gravel and is a perfect setting for a pot of zonal pelargoniums.

2

LEAN-TO CONSERVATORY

Linking house and garden, a lean-to conservatory provides the right degree of shelter and warmth for an extended range of more tender plants.

4

PAVED TERRACE

Bright new bricks can be chosen for the paved terrace for a look of graphic precision or old, worn bricks for a more mellow, rustic appeal.

CONTAINER GARDEN

···

Every space in this tiny garden is filled with a mass of colourful, fragrant flowers and foliage. An atmosphere of scent and beauty pervades, particularly in summer when everything is at its best. A curved wooden bench (apparent only when you are in the garden) allows you to sit among all the flowers. A trellised wall is covered with climbers; and diverse pots, planters and high-standing jardinières all enhance the visual effect. The white background shows up the plants to great advantage, and also makes the area seem a lot larger and brighter than it really is.

❶ CURVED BENCH

The curved bench in this tiny garden, hidden in a profusion of fragrant flowers and foliage, makes it possible to linger there in peace and contemplation.

❷ BRIGHT FLOWERS IN POTS

All kinds of pots, planters and high-standing jardinières to raise plants to different levels can be filled with petunias, pelargoniums, chrysanthemums and tobacco plants, to provide a mass of colour and fill the air with fragrance.

❸ TRELLIS

Trellised walls support a wealth of climbing plants, smothering the garden with flowers – clematis, jasmine, honeysuckle, Hydrangea petiolaris, along with climbers like Virginia creeper and Hedera 'Goldheart' for foliage colour and variety.

CONTAINER GARDEN

PONDS

Whatever its shape – regular or irregular, round, oblong or square – whatever its size – large

or small, grand or more modest – and wherever you put it – slap in the centre of the patio or

tucked away at the bottom of the rockery – a pond always adds an extra dimension of interest

to a garden. Water sets a peaceful atmosphere, while providing added interest in the mirror

images it creates of its surroundings and the changing patterns and colours of the sky.

IF YOU have a natural stream or spring in your garden, you're one of the fortunate ones. Most of us aren't that lucky and we have to start from scratch. However, the range of equipment and ready-made accessories for the new pond owner is wide indeed. Electrical pumps, underwater lighting and a wide variety of styles and designs of fountains are easy to find.

Waterfalls and fountains can be added to ponds to provide extra interest, and a variety of water plants and fish can make them fascinating features.

Flexible liners

WITH A flexible liner, you have much more choice when it comes to the shape of your pond since the material will stretch or fold to match practically any shape you care to invent. The weight of the water will make it hold its shape, the top edges being retained by paving slabs or stone.

A flexible pond liner is supplied as a flat sheet, and all you have to do is add twice the depth of the pond to its width and to its length to obtain the dimensions of the sheet you require. If your dimensions do not quite match those of a standard size sheet, simply buy the next size up.

TYPES OF LINER

• Rigid liners are made from fibreglass in a fairly wide range of shapes and sizes. They are very tough and virtually leakproof.

• Semi-rigid liners are made of vacuum-formed plastic. They are cheaper than rigid types of liner but are nowhere near as strong. You would probably be better off using a flexible liner.

• Flexible liners may be made from PVC reinforced with nylon or from butyl rubber. Of the two, the rubber version is the stronger and will often be guaranteed for 20 years, although it may last much longer than that – perhaps as long as 50 years.

LINER INSTALLATION

1 Mark out the pool and dig down in even layers. Span the excavation with a plank and measure to the depth of the floor.

2 Using a plasterer's trowel, plaster the excavation with a 2.5cm (1in) layer of damp sand, making sure it adheres well to the walls.

3 Lay the piece of liner over the excavation, making sure it is centred. Anchor the liner with stones around the edge of the pool.

4 Fill the pool with water. The liner will stretch into the shape of the excavation as it fills; gradually lift the stones in order to release the liner.

PRE-FORMED POOL INSTALLATION

1 Lay a good layer of damp sand on the floor of the excavation. This will serve as a cushion for the pre-formed pool unit.

2 Once it is installed, check that the unit is level by spanning it with a plank of wood and laying a spirit level on the plank.

3 Using a hose pipe, fill the unit with approximately 10cm (4in) of water before backfilling around the edges of the unit.

4 Work your way around the pool, feeding in a small quantity of material. After each circuit, check the unit level.

SITING YOUR POOL

- A formal rectangular or round pool will probably look best as the central feature of a paved patio rather than a lawn.
- An informal, natural-looking pool should be at the lowest point of your garden, since water always drains toward a low point.
- A pool should receive plenty of daylight, so do not put it where it is in constant shade.
- Do not put it under trees if you intend to keep fish in it. The falling leaves will sink to the bottom and decompose, giving off a poison that will kill fish.
- A pump for a waterfall or fountain will require running an electrical cable to the house.
- The pool should be on level ground, but if your garden slopes you can overcome this by digging away the ground on the up-slope side and holding it back with a retaining wall.

MAKING A BOG GARDEN

The bog garden should be constructed at the same time as the pool, using one large piece of liner for both features.

Excavate a 30cm (12in) basin next to the pool. Its edges must be the same height or a little higher than the bank of the pool, but the interconnecting lip must be a little lower. Spread a layer of coarse grit or gravel over the soil in order to aid drainage.

When the pool is lined, continue the liner over the lowered bank and across the bog area, and then tuck in the edges in the same way as for the pool. Puncture the liner in a few places and cover the floor with a layer of gravel to prevent the holes becoming clogged up. Add a layer of well-rotted farmyard manure before filling the basin with a mixture of loam and leafmould.

POOLS AND CHILDREN

If you have young children or pets, it may be better to build a raised pool. Do not have a pool with an overhanging rim with deep water below. Instead have a shallow 'beach' of pebbles in a more natural-looking pool; in a formal edged pool, probably the easiest solution is to place bricks or blocks near the edge just below the surface of the water to form steps.

Fountains

ANOTHER ATTRACTIVE water feature is a fountain which, like a waterfall, is operated by a submersible pump sitting on the floor of the pool, or on a platform of bricks or blocks if the pool is deep. Indeed, some pumps combine a fountain with a flexible hose outlet that can feed a waterfall as well.

Choosing a fountain

The important thing is to choose a fountain that will not overpower the effect of your pool. It should not shoot its jets so high that wind-blown spray falls outside the pool, nor should it be over-elaborate if the pool is small. Fountains are ideal for formal pools but should not be included in those that are supposed to look natural – the two just don't go together.

Installing a fountain

In most cases the fountain outlet simply projects above the pump and it can usually be fitted with a range of fountain heads that vary the pattern of the water jets. The pump should be positioned so that the head just projects above the level of the water in the pool, if necessary raised on a piece of paving.

RIGHT: fountains can look wonderful in this kind of formal setting.

Electric pumps

THE WATER for the waterfall is circulated by a submersible electric pump which usually takes its power from a transformer connected to the normal mains electricity supply.

Water is delivered to the top of the waterfall by a hose connected to the pump. Conceal this underground alongside the waterfall with its open end hidden by a rock.

The power cable for the pump sits on the floor of the pool. Run it under one of the edging stones and then take it to a waterproof connector and link it to the transformer with a cable. Although the low-voltage electricity carried by the cable between pump and transformer will not give you a serious electric shock, you should take steps to protect the cable from accidental damage. Do not leave it lying on the ground where, if nothing else, it could trip someone up, and do not run it along a fence which might be blown over.

By far the best idea is to run it through a plastic conduit about 600mm (24in) underground, making sure it is where you won't be digging in the future. This will provide total protection.

INSTALLING PUMPS

Simple fountains
Place the pump in the pool, on a piece of paving if necessary, to bring it up to the required height.

Ornamental fountains
Connect the pump to the fountain jet. If the fountain plinth is hollow, hide the pump inside it.

DECKING

A raised timber deck provides you with space outdoors for dozing, dining or soaking up

the sun, and can be constructed using just a few specialist carpentry techniques. Decorate the

surface with containers.

Planning the structure

DECIDE WHAT you are likely to use the deck for, as this helps you determine its overall size: if you intend to dine outdoors, it must be large enough for a table and chairs with space for people to pass behind when serving a meal. Where the deck will be used as a sunbathing area, space must be allowed for loungers. Decking combines best with timber fencing and wooden cask containers.

Consider how the deck will appear when attached to the house wall: if it is fairly narrow – say about 3m (10ft) – and projects out from the wall about 6m (20ft), it will not sit easily. A deck of this width running along the wall of the house would probably appear to be in better proportion. A squarer deck, on the other hand, is more in keeping with a corner location, set in the angle between two walls that meet at right-angles.

Draw a scale plan of the garden on graph paper and mark in the intended position and size of the deck, plus access arrangements and other features that might influence the design. Draw a side elevation of the site to illustrate the way the ground slopes: the deck can be constructed on sloping ground by adjusting the length of the timber posts so that the deck surface is horizontal.

Set up stringlines and pegs to mark the perimeter of the proposed deck so that you can imagine the visual impact it will have on the garden and the house.

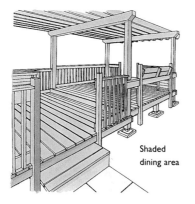

Shaded dining area

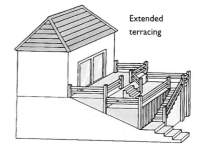

Extended terracing

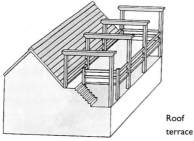

Roof terrace

TIMBER REQUIREMENTS

Use the plans you have drawn to work out the amount of timber needed. The main structural components are made from two stock sizes of timber: for the below-deck supports use 138 x 40mm (5½ x 1½ in) timber, with 75mm (3in) square timber for the above-deck supports. The deck joists should be made from 138 x 40mm (5½ x 1½ in) softwood, supporting slats of the same size timber laid flat rather than on edge.

THE BASIC DUCKBOARD

A basic timber slatted duckboard platform can be constructed entirely from lengths of preservative-treated sawn or planed softwood measuring about 75 x 25mm (3 x 1in) on a concrete surface. Assemble the duckboard on site. It is extremely straightforward to build, consisting of lengths of timber, which form the bearers, spanned by timber slats.

1 Space timber lengths about 760mm (30in) apart and parallel with each other running in the direction of the slope of the surface.

2 Cut slats of the same timber to span the width of the platform and place them across the bearers at right angles.

3 Set the slats about 5–15mm (¼–½ in) apart, using an offcut of wood as a spacer so that the gap is constant across the length.

4 Lay full lengths of timber across platforms up to 3m (10ft) wide. For wider platforms butt-join the lengths.

5 Stagger the joins at each side of the platform in alternate rows so that there are no continuous break lines.

6 Secure the slats to the bearers with 40mm (1½ in) long floorboard nails, two per bearer position.

The raised deck

RAISE THE deck on low brick walls or concrete piers about 30cm (1ft) high and spaced at about 1.2m (4ft) intervals across the site. Make sure there is some form of damp-proof course (such as bituminous felt) beneath the supports to prevent damp rising up through the brickwork and attacking the wood. For neatness, it is a good idea to build a continuous peripheral wall too, so that the underside of the deck is not accessible to pets and inquisitive small children. Make sure the tops of the walls are all level with each other as they provide the supports for the deck's main supporting joists. It is important that the surface of the deck remains at least 15cm (6in) below the house damp-proof course to prevent damp penetrating the walls.

Simply rest the joists on top of the low walls or concrete piers and construct the deck as previously described.

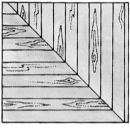
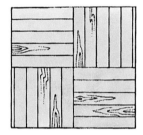
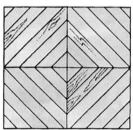
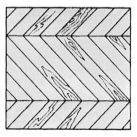

Attractive geometrical patterns can be formed by the decking (above). The more complex, intricate patterns may require more elaborate supports. Some of the options available include chequerboard (top right), angled chequerboard (bottom left), concentric rectangles (top left), and traditional herringbone (bottom right). In some situations it is preferable to consider using a simple arrangement of parallel slats, perhaps laid on a diagonal in relation to the adjacent house wall, to give a dynamic effect.

LEFT:

**simple and
effective decking
formed of single
slats.**

ABOVE:

joists can be
laid in a simple
square pattern
(bottom) or a
diagonal pattern
(centre).
For more
complex designs,
use extra strong
diagonal joists *(top).*

PLANT ASSOCIATIONS

Whichever plants we choose to grow, they must be displayed well if they are to look their best. The easiest way to group is to make a series of small garden 'pictures' and create clusters of plants, sometimes only two or three, each adding to the others' beauty and effectiveness.

Shape, height and texture

PLANT ASSOCIATION is not just a question of putting together plants that flower at the same time. Instead, look for plants that complement each other in terms of habit and size, texture and colour.

Shape

All plants fall into one of a number of basic shape categories, the plants in each category fulfilling a similar role in the overall scheme. There is the tall upright shape of fastigiate trees and conifers which leads the eye upwards and commands attention, especially when used repeatedly in a group or row. The effect is the same whatever the scale. Low rounded shapes

RIGHT: colour and shape complement each other in this match of pyrethrum and foxgloves.

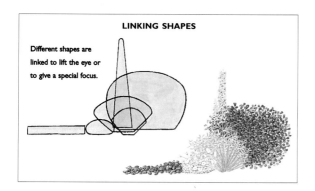

Consider the basic shape categories of plants when planning the garden.

LINKING SHAPES

Different shapes are linked to lift the eye or to give a special focus.

or domes are equally arresting, but in a more earthbound way. They sit heavily upon the ground and fix the eye. Fans or fountain shapes offer a softer touch, lifting the eye but in a gentler lighter way than a conifer. A more extreme version of this effect is the weeping shape, less visually static than the sphere and less busy than the fountain. Finally, there are the horizontal shapes. They keep the eye peacefully arrested, moving neither up nor down. There are endless variations within and between these categories, but when planning a layout they are very useful devices. As well as looking at the overall shape of a plant, do not forget to focus in on the form of its flowers. Choose flower shapes that complement one another in some way, either a combination of pleasing

ABOVE: the circular shape of *Allium giganteum* adds visual variety to any group of plants.

RIGHT: the unusual combination of penstemon and *Eryngium alpinum* makes a vivid contrast.
FAR RIGHT: *Euphorbia marginata* is grown for its unusual form and cactus-like texture.

contrasts or harmonious similarities. Remember, too, the shapes of individual leaves, and even the branch patterns of trees and shrubs.

Height

A variation in levels and a variation of plant heights all help to add interest to a border planting. The regularity of a border planted with tall plants at the back and low-growing ones at the front can be much more interesting if you introduce a few tall plants mid-way, to create some interest at intervals.

Texture

Plants not only have form, they also have texture: coarse or fine, solid or filigree, and so on. Some are velvety soft to touch while others are hard and unyielding; some absorb light and some reflect it.

Texture is perhaps best appreciated from a distance. Create patterns using different textures: plant a misty open plant against a dense, solid plant; try mixing hostas and ferns, for example.

USING FOLIAGE

Foliage plays a vital role in the garden, for not only does it create a neutral backdrop against which colourful flowers will show up, but it has a much longer period of interest than flowers and berries and so forms the framework of your planting. Indeed, evergreen leaves are a good way of providing year-round interest.

Foliage is particularly useful for texture, and there is no better way of breaking up blocks of colour than by introducing leafy plants. There are many types whose leaves are hand-some in shape, agreeable in colour and pleasing in texture.

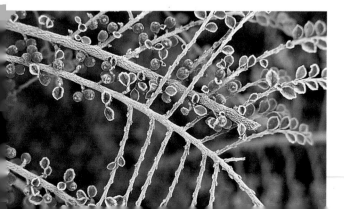

OPPOSITE: colour, texture and foliage are all elements that are skilfully combined in this mixed border.

ABOVE: the bold ornamental *Eryngium alpinum* is a handsome sight in a large garden.

LEFT: the spare outline of branches can be an attractive counterpoint to other plants.

Year-round interest

A GARDEN CAN never be as colourful in winter as in summer, but there is no reason why it should not be just as interesting, though in different ways. This is simply a matter of planning so that your garden has some framework plants (preferably evergreen) to give year-round interest and there is always something attractive to look at. Each season needs thinking about in terms of the colour of flowers, foliage and fruit, form, texture, perfume, and the uses to which the garden will be put. Even if summer colour is desired, it is still possible to underplant and interplant for other times of the year using bulbs and annuals.

Bulbs and annuals are invaluable for spring and early summer colour, while herbaceous perennials are the most colourful summer contributors. In many places herbaceous perennials can be found in flower for most of the year, and by planting a good cross section it is possible to get a long flowering season.

Autumn colour can be found in trees like maples and rowans, but there are vines of equal brilliance and even herbaceous plants such as euphorbia and gillenia. Fruits and berries need not just be an autumn feature. Many roses carry their hips and *Mahonia aquifolium* bears its blue berries in late summer. Later come the reds, yellows and oranges of holly (*Ilex*), rowans (*Sorbus aucuparia*), cotoneasters and pyracantha. Usually the paler the berries,

the later the birds will descend to eat them.

Colour in the garden in winter may seem impossible, until you realize that there are plants for which winter is the natural time of flowering. Certainly you will not get a great deal of bloom, but you will find a surprising variety of plants that will take up where the summer plants left off, and flower in succession through the otherwise dormant months of the year. Such shrubs as witch hazel (*Hamamelis*), some

of the rhododendrons, cotylopis and *Mahonia* 'Charity', and herbaceous perennials, hellebores, snowdrops, *Iris reticulata*, bergenias and some of the violets are all winter-flowering.

To add to winter colour, there is a great variety of textures and colours to choose from including: the glossy spiny leaves of holly, the soft gold of some variegated yews, or the blue of spruce needles. The interest supplied by coloured bark is also invaluable. Stooled dogwoods

BELOW: a cool backdrop for colourful plants is provided by the soft green shapes of ferns.

offer scarlet, purple and yellow bark; while that of willows is orange, grey or glossy brown. Some species of birch have brilliant white or coppery-pink bark and there are cherries with the glorious, dramatic bark of purest polished mahogany.

In winter a garden falls back on its structure to make itself interesting, and it is then that the most benefit is gained from light and shade and the clarity of the design. With careful plant choice, your garden can continue to be clothed in winter – in fact, a really well-designed and thought-out garden will look just as good, though in a different way, as in summer.

Scent

HAVING SATISFIED the eye by planting subjects of good form and colour, do not forget to include some scented plants. Aromatic plants add an extra dimension. Scented carpet plants like thyme and camomile can be planted in the gaps between paving and will release their fragrance when brushed against. Lavender alongside paths will scent the air, as will perfumed roses and certain border plants.

Colour

COLOUR IS without doubt the most obvious part of an ornamental plant's attraction, and the most important to the majority of gardeners. A dazzling, riotous display of colour from spring to autumn is generally the ideal for beginner gardeners. But as time goes on and experience accumulates, this aim gradually

ABOVE: the bright yellow of *Hypericum* 'Hidcote' has a bold summer presence.

changes as you realize that more subtle but more satisfying blendings can be obtained, in which colour is mixed with white, or cool greys and silvers, or with plants grown for the shape and texture of their leaves.

A blaze of all the colours of the rainbow is difficult to absorb all at once: much better to group the plants in types of colour, and merge each into the one adjacent to it. Pink, purple, rose, grey, lavender, blue and lilac make one group; and yellow, cream, orange, bronze, brown and light red another. The reds will graduate into shades of rose, lavender and so to blue; or on the opposite side into scarlet, vermilion, flame and finally yellow. Grey-leafed and white-flowered plants will calm down the brighter colours, and mix beautifully with muted shades.

Another way of breaking up blocks of colour is to introduce leafy plants. There are many species whose leaves are handsome in shape, agreeable in colour and pleasing in texture. These deserve a place in the garden in their own right.

LEFT: the green and white foliage of hostas makes a cool colour combination together with white tulips.

RIGHT: a modern pink shrub rose, 'Rosy Cushion', cascades over a pink and blue border.

BELOW: a bold colour scheme of scarlet 'Toronto' tulips, blue muscari and pink rhododendrons.

Colour wheel

ALTHOUGH THE PERCEPTION of colour and taste is a personal and subjective matter, there are basic guidelines that can help you plan the colour schemes of your garden.

The theory behind colour combinations, both harmonies and contrasts, can be most readily understood by visualizing a chart known as the colour wheel. This is based on the colours of the spectrum and consists of the primary colours red, blue and yellow, separated by the secondary, blended colours violet, green and orange. Colours adjacent to each other on the wheel, such as yellow and orange or blue and green, are generally considered to go well together – in other words they harmonize. Colours opposite each other, however, such as red and green or blue and orange, can be seen as contrasting colours, known as complementary colours. There are, of course, infinite nuances of colour between each of these rather artificial subdivisions of the wheel. Colours can be pale or intense depending on the colours they are mixed with and, technically speaking, they become shades, tints and tones of the original base colour. A shade, for instance, is created by adding black to the base colour, while a tint is made by adding white, and a tone is the result of a colour being either lightened or darkened by the addition of grey.

RIGHT: the glorious reds of Virginia creeper enrich the autumn garden.
BELOW: the rich purple of clematis is a summer favourite.

LEFT AND BELOW: adjoining colours on the wheel blend happily, as with these yellow/red tulips *(left)* and the bright yellow of *Zinnia elegans (below)*.

ABOVE AND RIGHT: purple-blue violas *(above)* at ground level harmonize with the heavenly blue of the climber *Ipomoea* or morning glory *(right)*.

LEFT: the handsome ornamental foliage of the hardy evergreen *Ilex* 'Golden King' makes a telling contrast with bold primary reds.

shades of pink and
blue combine happily
– a mixture of
Allium sphaerocephalon
and phlox.

ABOVE: use bright
colours in small
touches of brilliance
for the best effect.

Such variations make a huge difference to the effect of colour combinations; different intensities of one basic colour create a completely different feel. Take an apparently simple association of blue and yellow. Pale blue and pale yellow is a soft, unchallenging combination with a restful and airy feel to it. Now consider a mixture of golden yellow and violet blue and you have a far more vibrant and challenging effect which makes much more of a statement. However, both combinations have a place in the garden, the pale planting being particularly appropriate in a corner of an old walled garden for a timeless, relaxed atmosphere, and the stronger scheme being perfect as part of a mixed planting along a path to promote the feeling of movement.

Colours can also be loosely divided into warm and cool effects, with greens and greys providing a neutral buffer zone in between. Reds, oranges and golden yellows seem warm, while purples and blues seem cooler. Furthermore, warm shades appear to advance towards the eye, making an area seem smaller than it really is, while cool colours seem to recede, thereby providing the illusion of space. In practice, if you clothe a garden in cool and light colours it will seem bigger than in reality, which is useful in small gardens, and to make large gardens more intimate, you can interrupt a view and bring the eye up short with a strong display of bright, warm colours.

Experimenting with these effects is immensely enjoyable and the only way of developing your individual garden style. Do not be afraid of making mistakes, but it can be a good idea to try out colour combinations with bulbs or bedding plants first, before investing time and money in planting shrubs and perennials.

CREATING A BORDER

The wonderful thing about gardening is that you are free to
create as you wish. Lovers of shrubs can establish a shrub
border, while wonderful spot beds can be made with annuals;
and roses can be really spectacular when they are grouped
together. But surely the most interesting sight of all in the
garden must be the flower border that provides a little bit of
everything – annuals, perennials, shrubs, bulbs and roses.

BELOW:
a well-established
cottage garden
border – a mixture
of achillea, campanula
and scabiosa.

MOST PEOPLE call it the mixed border, although 'versatile' might be a far better word because it suggests both colourful flowers and attractive foliage right through the year. Certainly the mixed border must rank as the most rewarding feature of the small to average-sized garden. The possibilities are enormous. Just consider growing sweet peas side by side with an elegant group of regal lilies, or having dramatic large-flowered delphiniums towering over old-fashioned pinks, all close beside the soft-coloured bearded iris.

A border of mixed or herbaceous plants will provide flowers and foliage for cutting, and plants that can be left in position for a number of years. Apart from pruning and dividing, they demand little work. However, it has to be said that these benefits will only be reaped by those who put the initial work into the planning, designing and preparing. That might sound horrifying to the new gardener, but it can be a pleasure.

Such a border can be planted anywhere, even in open lawn, although where it can be viewed from each side there will be more restrictions on the types of plants you can use. Most usually a background wall, fence or hedge will provide the necessary frame, and will also provide a windbreak, which is important when taller plants are being grown.

The dedicated planner can devise a highly scented border devoted to one type of plant (such as the rose), or a theme – delphiniums, dahlias, chrysanthemums and roses, among those that immediately

ABOVE: long-flowering petunias – equally at home in the garden or in pots and baskets.

come to mind, but there are so many others that the gardener can be spoilt for choice.

A scented garden has its own obvious pleasures, and despite the cries that scent is being lost by modern flower breeders there are many different types of flowers that can be used effectively in this way. The heady scent of wallflowers *Erysimum*, the lovely mignonette and, of course, night-scented-stock are all excellent choices. There are many more that can be appreciated from spring to winter, and they include the white *Nicotiana* (tobacco plant) and many forms of lilac, lavender, lily-of-the-valley, honeysuckle, viburnum, sweet peas and jasmine.

Size and shape

A BORDER needs a certain amount of space to be effective. The minimum requirements are 1.2 x 3.7m (4 x 12ft). If the border is any smaller than this you should restrict the number

of plants used to six or seven different types, ensuring that they provide a good mix of flowers and foliage over a long period of the year.

If you have more space it is possible to create one of a wide range of borders, incorporating varying widths and curves, which will be far more interesting than a border of straight lines. One of the great advantages of a mixed or herbaceous border is that you can change it from year to year. And as you become more adventurous and knowledgeable, it will be possible for you to create bolder and ever more spectacular border displays.

Introducing plants

WHEN DESIGNING a border, never think of a plant in isolation: judge it as a companion for its neighbours. Plants should always be positioned to show one another off, not simply planted in the soil. Rely on leaf shape, colour and texture even more than on flowers. The leaves are in evidence for most of the year (all year if they are ever-green), whereas flowers are fleeting. You will find that almost all flowers have more impact if they are shown off by a back-drop of handsome foliage than if they have to sit in mid-air. Also choose your plants with seasons of interest in mind. Make sure there is at least a handful of flowers, fruits and bright foliage to see you through the winter until the colourful spring show begins once more and the garden comes alive.

Flowering shrubs can be used to provide a permanent framework in the border and a setting for perennials, annuals and bulbs with their more flamboyant flowers. Many will also create year-round interest with fruits following flowers, silver or evergreen foliage and fiery autumn colour. The choice of perennials is almost without bounds but once you have selected your favourites, and once they are established, they will go on growing and flowering for several seasons, giving pleasure year after year.

Annuals are superb for bringing colour into mixed borders. Either use them boldly spread in drifts, so that their colour is not diluted, or mix them with other plants and perhaps plant them by scale rather than by colour. There is a wide range of bulbous plants that can be grown in a mixed border, from the stately gladiolus to the perfumed lily. Make sure that you know the eventual height that the flower will reach before planting it.

ABOVE: **during this border's first year, annuals and tender plants complement the permanent planting.**

BELOW: **by late spring, the peony and barberries are in full bloom, and white arabis flowers in the foreground.**

ABOVE: a subtle border combination of rose, phlomis, lily and *Allium caeruleum*.

PRACTICALITIES

Some of the rules for creating a mixed border are:

• All borders, whether shrub or mixed, need sun, so must be sited in the sunniest part of the garden.

• Careful soil preparation is vital. There is nothing to beat a well-dug, fertilized bed.

• If planting against a wall, hedge or fence, leave at least 45cm (18in) between the back of the border and the 'frame'. If you can, lay some sort of path. This will make it easy for you to tend to the back of the border and to repair the wall or fence, or trim the hedge.

• Soggy land or a sunless position are the two great handicaps. Try for good drainage and full sun.

• When selecting plants make sure that you have allowed space for those that are rampant growers and which may suffocate slower-growing plants placed near them.

• Place taller-growing plants (such as weigela or fuchsia) at the back of the border, with the lower ones in front. The middle area is reserved for the iris, lupin, stocks and other average-sized flowers.

• Try to keep the ground between plants open by hoeing and weeding.

• A mulch of organic material – peat or well-rotted compost, for instance – will keep down weeds and also conserve water. On the edges of beds a mulch of small forest bark can be very effective.

• When cutting flowers for house decoration be gentle on new plants. The loss of stems and greenery can harm next year's growth. This will be obvious on perennials and even newly planted roses. If you want a flower from a first-year plant, then cut it with as little stem as possible.

• Remove flower heads once they have faded, which will give the plants a chance of repeat flowering later in the season. Remove them with sharp scissors, shears or secateurs.

• If you wish to move a plant in the border wait until autumn, but identify where to place it.

• Wear gloves. These can be awkward to work in but they are safer.

Putting your thoughts on paper

IT IS OFTEN helpful, in the planning stages of a border, to make simple sketches that block in the most important shapes and lines (as well as the main colour effects). This will enable you to envisage the composition in advance and allows the main refinements to be made before planting begins. It is also useful for considering the mature aspect of the garden at different seasons, which should include appropriate spacing of trees and large shrubs at their ultimate size. This is an excellent tool for clarifying your ideas; on paper, the imagination can run riot, but once planting begins, changes become much more difficult. A plan can bring you that much closer to your ideal,

ABOVE: this spring border contains bulbs supplemented by wallflowers and forget-me-nots.

LEFT: in summer perennials take over from the bulbs and harmonize with the foliage of the juniper and euphorbia.

ABOVE: the splendid golden yellow *Achillea filipendulina* is ideal for border planting.

well-balanced garden. With the outline in hand, start filling in planting details on the plan – shapes, colours, texture and scent, leaving the choice of most plants until last.

The next stage is to ensure that the planting line-up is going to provide colour and interesting shapes right through the year. Use four different-coloured pens (signifying winter, spring, summer and autumn) to mark blocks of plants on the plan and, if possible, grow one spectacular plant for every season in each area. (When planting, leave space around the young specimens to accommodate their ultimate spread. Annuals and bedding plants can be used to fill the gaps temporarily.)

Planning a border

THE BEST WAY of planning a border is to work with small groups of plants so you can concentrate on the relationship between the subjects, and so gradually build up the groups into a whole border planting. Choose plants with shapes that complement each other and which make an interesting and varied effect.

You will notice that different plants create a variety of effects. Spiky plants, for example, are active and lead the eye upwards and onwards to neighbouring plants, while gentle hummock-forming plants are calming and bland, and lead the eye horizontally along the border.

At the same time think of height. Either use a tier system with tall plants at the back and shorter ones at the front, or use tall plants in the middle of the group to create peaks of interest, with shorter-growing plants leading the eye upwards towards them. This will divert the eye and prevent it from travelling straight down the border, taking it all in at a glance. However, if tall plants are used towards the front of a border, they should be wispy enough to allow the eye to pass through them, yet substantial enough to break the line.

LEFT: a brilliant border of narcissi, blue Anemone blanda and tall *Fritillaria imperialis*.

BELOW AND BELOW LEFT: planting plan for a mixed border containing a combination of plant heights and shapes.

KEY

1. *Alchemilla mollis* (z4–8)
2. *Ajuga reptans* 'Atropurpurea' (z3–8)
3. *Dianthus* 'Mrs Sinkins' (z4–8)
4. *Iris pallida* 'Argentea Variegata' (z4–9)
5. *Lavandula angustifolia* 'Munstead' (z6–9)
6. *Sisyrinchium striatum* (z7–8)
7. *Sedum spectabile* (z4–9)
8. *Geranium clarkei* 'Kashmir White' (z4–8)
9. *Heuchera micrantha* 'Palace Purple' (z4–8)
10. *Salvia nemorosa* 'Ostfriesland' (z5–9)
11. *Achillea* 'Moonshine' (z4–8)
12. *Aster thomsonii* 'Nanus' (z5–8)
13. *Catananche caerulea* (z5–8)
14. *Lavandula* x *intermedia* 'Grappenhall' (z8–9)
15. *Santolina chamaecyparissus* (z6–9)
16. *Agapanthus* Headbourne hybrids (z8–10)
17. *Spiraea japonica* 'Goldflame' (z4–9)
18. *Aster novi-belgii* 'Marie Ballard' (z4–8)
19. *Aster novi-belgii* 'White Ladies' (z4–8)
20. *Anemone* x *hybrida* 'Queen Charlotte' (z6–8)
21. *Euphorbia characias wulfenii* (z7–10)
22. *Delphinium* Pacific hybrids (z2–9)
23. *Cotinus coggygria* 'Royal Purple' (z5–9)
24. *Echinops ritro* (z4–9)
25. *Berberis thunbergii atropurpurea* (z5–9)
26. *Aster novae-angliae* 'Harrington's Pink' (z4–8)

WAYS WITH ROSES

There are few places in a garden, however small, that cannot be enhanced by roses. Ground-cover types brighten the soil with flowers, pillar roses stand like sentries and create colour throughout much of summer, standard roses add height to rose beds, while miniature and patio types can be introduced into even the smallest area of courtyard or balcony. Climbers and ramblers cover walls and fences and some are ideal for growing as flowering hedges.

ABOVE: everyone loves red roses – like the intensely red *R. gallica* 'Duc de Guiche'.

ABOVE: enveloping trelliswork, pink blooms of the Bourbon climber, 'Old Rectory'.

RIGHT: in the foreground, the shrub rose 'Pink Grootendorst', which is highly recommended for cutting and including in your flower arrangements.

Bush roses

BUSH ROSES usually form the main part of a rose garden. The term refers to Hybrid Teas (correctly known as Large-flowered roses) and Floribundas (correctly known as Cluster-flowered roses).

Hybrid Teas produce the largest and most beautifully formed blooms of all and they have a colour range that lacks only blue and deep black. They are also highly scented, but their greatest glory comes from their ability to produce continuous crops of flowers from early summer to mid-winter. Where they grow in the garden is best decided by you. Grow them in a group on their own or in a mixed border.

Floribundas have clusters of flowers which look much more informal than Hybrid Teas. For impact, they are best grown in beds of one type although they can also be placed in mixed borders.

Climbers and ramblers

CLIMBERS CAN transform a garden with flourishes of colour. They are superb for covering house walls, framing windows and doors, climbing up pillars, arches and pergolas, as well as scrambling into trees. Climbers have a more permanent framework than ramblers, and their flowers range from small to those as large as Hybrid Teas. Ramblers have huge trusses carrying hundreds of generally small blooms, but there is only one truss of flowers. They are excellent for growing in tall trees.

ABOVE: the rampant rambler 'Caroline Testoyt'.

KEY PLANNING POINTS

• With bedding roses, plant the taller varieties in the centre.

• Stagger the planting within a bed.

• Keep the roses at least 45cm (18in) from the outside edges of the beds to avoid problems when trimming the grass.

• Do not make the bed any deeper than 1.5m (5ft), otherwise you will have difficulty reaching and cutting off dead heads.

• The same points apply to borders and to beds, except that as the roses are not being seen from all sides the tallest (like 'Queen Elizabeth' and 'Alexander') should be at the back, medium-sized growers in the centre, and low growers in the front row.

• Try to plant roses in batches of three to five to form a group of one colour.

• Some roses make good hedges, but do check the height and colour before you place your order.

• There are many different roses, such as the patio types 'Sweet Dreams', 'Sweet Magic' and 'Cider Cup', and the older 'Ballerina' with its five-petalled blooms of light pink and white eye, which are ideal for planting in tubs and urns.

GROWTH TYPES

Prostrate rose 30–38cm
(12–15in) (or less)

Miniature bush
38cm (15in) (or less)

Miniature standard
20–30cm (8–12in) (stem)

Patio rose 38cm (15in)

Dwarf bush 45–60cm
(18–24in)

Bush rose 60cm (24in)
(or more)

Half-standard 75cm
(2½ ft) (stem)

Shrub roses

SHRUB ROSES is an all-embracing classification that covers a huge range of roses including Species and Old roses, such as Bourbon, China, Damask, Moss and Tea types. These roses are mostly big, heavy-petalled and perfumed, available in wonderful colours.

Miniature and patio roses

THESE FASCINATING roses have small flowers and a miniature stature suitable for, among other things, edging borders, planting in rock gardens and planting in containers. There are also dwarf

Full standard 1m (39in) (stem)

Weeping standard 1.3m
(51in) (stem)

Pillar rose 2.1–2.4m (7–8 ft)

polyantha roses characterized by their bushy, compact habit.

Flower colours

TERMS USED to describe the colours of flowers include:
• Single colour: one colour
• Bi-colour: the colours on the inside and outside of each petal are different
• Blend: two or more colours on each petal
• Multi-coloured: colours change with age
• Hand-painted: centre is light-coloured and delicately feathered merging with other colours towards the outside
• Striped: two or more colours positioned in bands or stripes

Miniature Climber 1.2–1.8m (4–6ft)

Climber 2.1–9m (7–30ft) (or more)

Rambler 2.1–9m (7–30ft) (or more)

Flowering times

ROSES FLOWER over a surprisingly long period during summer, some just once, others repeatedly.

Single flush, also known as 'once flowering', refers to roses that generally have only one flowering period, usually in the latter part of early summer and into mid-summer and lasting for several weeks. Occasionally a few flowers appear later, but not sufficient to create a spectacular display. However, there are some ramblers and shrub roses which flower in late spring, early summer or late summer.

Repeat-flowering is also known as 'recurrent and 'remontant'; these roses have two or more flushes of flowers a year. Where a variety produces flowers between the main flushes, these are known as 'perpetual' and 'continuous' flowering, but these terms can create a false impression about the flowering period, which is neither perpetual nor continuous, though it still gives good value.

ABOVE: 'Frau Dagmar Hastrup' has single shell-pink flowers, is very fragrant and repeat-flowering. Often grown as a hedge, it has large red hips in the autumn.

LEFT: the creamy-white semi-double blooms of 'Nevada' smother the whole bush, hiding the leaves and thornless red stems. It needs plenty of space.

RIGHT: not truly blue, the variety 'Blue Moon' is more a shade of lilac. The full double flower of many petals is very fragrant and the blooms look their best indoors in a vase.

LEFT: 'Pascali' has a good reputation for being more resistant to rain than most white roses and the blooms hold their shape. The stems are long and straight and good for cutting.

RIGHT: 'National Trust' is an outstanding crimson Hybrid Tea rose, excellent for the front of the bed or border. The blooms are held erect and their colour does not fade. The foliage is coppery red when young.

FAVOURITE CLIMBING ROSES (z4–9)

'Albertine'
(pinkish-white;
scented)

'Mme Alfred
Carrière'
(creamy-white; highly scented)

'Mme Grégoire Staechelin'
(clear pink shaded carmine)

'New Dawn' (pearl-pink; fragrant)

'Parkdirektor Riggers'
(deep crimson; fragrant)

HIGHLY SCENTED ROSES (z4–9)

'Fantin-Latour' (pink climber)

'Gloire de Dijon'
(buff-coloured climber)

'Mme Hardy' (white climber or shrub)

'Mme Isaac Pereire'
(pink climber or shrub)

'Zéphirine Drouhin' (pink climber)

ABOVE: the lovely 'Albertine' is an old favourite, a climber with fragrance.

BELOW LEFT: an unusual English-bred modern shrub rose, the striking, deep yellow 'Graham Thomas'.

ABOVE: 'Ruby Wedding', a deep red rose for the small garden or the front of the border, popular as a celebration gift.

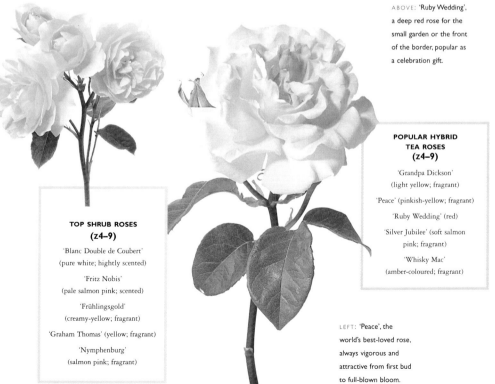

POPULAR HYBRID TEA ROSES (z4–9)

'Grandpa Dickson'
(light yellow; fragrant)

'Peace' (pinkish-yellow; fragrant)

'Ruby Wedding' (red)

'Silver Jubilee' (soft salmon
pink; fragrant)

'Whisky Mac'
(amber-coloured; fragrant)

TOP SHRUB ROSES (z4–9)

'Blanc Double de Coubert'
(pure white; hightly scented)

'Fritz Nobis'
(pale salmon pink; scented)

'Frühlingsgold'
(creamy-yellow; fragrant)

'Graham Thomas' (yellow; fragrant)

'Nymphenburg'
(salmon pink; fragrant)

LEFT: 'Peace', the world's best-loved rose, always vigorous and attractive from first bud to full-blown bloom.

BEST OLD-FASHIONED ROSES

'Charles de Mills' (crimson-maroon;
fragrant) (z4–9)

'Ispahan' (clear pink) (z4–9)

'Mousseline' (blush-pink) (z4–9)

moschata (clear pink) (z6–9)

gallica 'Versicolor' (pale pink with
crimson stripes; fragrant) (z5–9)

ABOVE: Bold and bright
'Stars 'n' Stripes' is
universally recognized
for its strawberry red
stripes against white.

ABOVE: yellow climbing roses
such as 'Golden Showers' have
great appeal for their deep
golden colour and their long
flowering period.

ABOVE: the blooms of
'Silver Jubilee' are shapely
with long, coppery pink
petals, shaded with peach.

LEFT: one of the best of
the old-fashioned roses,
'Ispahan', a clear pink.

SHRUBS FOR YEAR-ROUND INTEREST

Shrubs of all kinds make a year-long contribution to the garden scene. They can be planted on their own, in groups or with herbaceous plants.

BELOW: shrubs, deciduous and evergreen, can be mixed to provide continuous colour and variety in the garden.

EVEN THE deciduous kinds of shrub (for example, *Buddleja davidii* and *Hydrangea macrophylla*), which lose their leaves in the autumn, have interesting branch patterns. These are sometimes given added attraction by virtue of having a particularly distinctive bark colour.

Evergreen shrubs (like *Viburnum tinus* and *Ceanothus impressus*) retain their leaves all winter and then stand out in sharp contrast to the deciduous kinds, which should be taken into account when deciding where to locate them. Evergreens that have leaves variegated with white or cream (*Euonymus fortunei* 'Silver Queen')

or yellow (*Aucuba japonica*) can be particularly valuable in the winter months because they add a touch of colour.

Some shrubs are grown primarily for the beauty of their flowers (*Syringa x persica*), some for their berries or other autumn fruits (*Cotoneaster x watereri*), some for the colour of their foliage (*Cotinus coggyria* 'Royal Purple'), and a few combine two or more of these attractions. There is also great variety in height and habit, from completely prostrate shrubs such as some species of cotoneaster, to almost tree-like specimens, such as the lilacs.

ABOVE: colour and fragrance combine perfectly in syringa (lilac), which thrives in a sunny position.

LEFT: *Hydrangea quercifolia* gives good value with its long-lasting flowers.

Using shrubs

SHRUBS ARE commonly grouped either with other shrubs or with herbaceous plants and annuals, but some kinds look their best planted as isolated specimens and some can be trained against walls. *Magnolia stellata* is an excellent example of the former type and pyracantha, Japanese quince (*Chaenomeles japonica*), and ceanothus all do well against walls, where their stiff branches may provide support for genuine climbers, such as the less rampant varieties of clematis. Most shrubs take several years to attain their full size. In the meantime, temporary plants, such as dahlias, annuals and herbaceous perennials, can be used to fill the space until the shrubs require it all.

ABOVE: viburnum is a hardy deciduous and evergreen shrub. Some varieties of viburnum have a pronounced fragrance.

BELOW: there are many excellent reasons for choosing shrubs: for their flowers, their berries and – perhaps most of all – for the beauty of their foliage.

FAVOURITE SHRUBS

Abelia x grandiflora (z6–9)
This shrub has arching branches of pointed, deep green leaves and small, very fragrant pink-tinged, white flowers. This is a useful shrub since it flowers well into autumn when little else is of interest. 'Goldsport' is a yellow-variegated form.

Buddleja davidii –
Butterfly bush (z5–8)
A favourite plant for attracting butterflies, buddlejas have long, conical spikes of flowers ranging in colour from deep purple ('Black Knight') to mauve ('Empire Blue') and white ('Peace').

Chaenomeles speciosa –
Ornamental quince (z5–9)
This colourful shrub produces bright vermilion-coloured flowers in early spring, sometimes followed by yellow fruits in autumn. 'Nivalis' has white flowers, 'Moerloesii' has pink and white flowers, while 'Simonii' has semi-double crimson flowers, which are ideal against walls.

Ceanothus impressus (z8–10)
This evergreen bush produces clusters of beautiful deep blue flowers from late spring right through to autumn.

Cornus alba – Red-barked dogwood (z2–8)
The young shoots are bright red in winter, while the dark green leaves turn vivid shades of orange and red in autumn. Creamy-white, star-shaped flowers are produced in spring. 'Elegantissima' has white-edged, grey-green leaves; 'Spaethii' has yellow-edged, green leaves.

Cotinus coggygria – Smoke tree (z5–9)
This neatly mounded shrub has rounded or oval leaves which turn red or yellow in autumn, and plumes of pale greyish-brown flowers. 'Royal Purple' has purple leaves and pink flowers.

Cotoneaster frigidus (z7–8)
Cotoneasters are grown
primarily for their red
autumnal berries, but they
are also fine evergreens. They
are very hardy.

Cytisus x praecox –
Warminster broom (z6–9)
In mid-spring this broom is
covered in a cascade of
yellow flowers.

Daphne odora (z7–9)
Daphnes are popular plants,
known for their rich heady
perfume and for their
beautiful pink, lilac and
white flowers.

Kerria japonica (z5–9)
This graceful shrub has golden-
yellow flowers on green shoots.

Magnolia stellata (z5–9)
The sweetly scented flowers
of this magnolia are white,
star-shaped and many-petalled.
The leaves are narrow and
deep green.

Syringa vulgaris (z3–8)
Lilacs have trusses of highly
scented flowers, which can be
white, cream, purple, mauve
or pink.

Viburnum x burkwoodii
(z4–8)
This shrub produces fragrant
pink then white flowers above
glossy, dark-green leaves. 'Park
Farm Hybrid' is very fragrant,
with dark-pink buds.

BELOW: **in summer cytisus is a brilliant display of yellow, with other varieties yellow/red and white.**

ABOVE: striking an unusual blue note in the garden.

CAMELLIAS (z7–9)

These evergreen shrubs are grouped according to flower type: single, semi-double, anemone-form, peony-form, rose-form, formal double and irregular double. These are produced above glossy green leaves. *C. japonica* 'Alba' has single white flowers with yellow centres; *C. j.* 'Rubescens Major' is a formal double with deep pink flowers; *C. j.* 'Mathotiana' has formal double red-pink flowers, *C* x *williamsii* 'Donation' is a semi-double with mid-pink flowers; *C.* x *w.* 'Clarrie Fawcett' has pale pink, semi-double flowers; and 'Anticipation', a peony type, has dark-pink flowers (pictured below).

ABOVE: **yellow-centred** *Camellia japonica* 'Alba'.

LEFT: **pale-pink** *Camellia* 'Donation'.

ABOVE: **red peony-flowered**
Camellia 'Anticipation'.

Acknowledgements

Leisuredeck Limited 19
Octopus Publishing Group Ltd./
Michael Boys 20, 21 left, 28 Top
Right, 31, 44 Top, 44 Bottom, 46
Right, 47 left, 47 Top, 47 Bottom
/Jerry Harpur 2, 23 Top, 24, 25, 28
centre right above, 28 centre right
below, 45 Top Left
/Neil Holmes 16

/Kelvin Murray 1
/Clive Nichols 22, 26, 27 Bottom,
29 Top, 30, 32, 35
/Guy Ryecart 39 Top, 39 Bottom,
40 left, 40 Top, 41 Bottom, 41
Bottom Left, 41 Bottom, 41 Top Left
/Steve Wooster 27 Top, 36 Top
Left, 36 Bottom Left, 36 Bottom
Right, 37, 41 Top Right, 42 Top

Left, 42 Top Right, 42 Bottom Left,
42 Bottom Right
/George Wright 21 right, 21
Centre, 23 Bottom, 28 Top Left, 28
Bottom, 28 centre left above, 28
centre left below, 29 Bottom, 34,
43, 46 left